A. ?

STOP NEGATIVE THINKING IN 7 EASY STEPS

7 Lessons & 7 Exercises for Beginners to Beat Pessimism

Understanding The Masters of Enlightenment:
Eckhart Tolle, Dalai Lama, Ramana Maharshi,
Krishnamurti and more!

THE SECRET OF NOW SERIES
GRAPEVINE BOOKS
Third Edition
2016

DISCLAIMER

AUTHOR: A. J. Parr
edicionesdelaparra@gmail.com

Cover Tolle photo by Kyle Hoobin (Creative Commons) See in Wikipedia
Cover painting: *"The Scream"* by Edward Munch.
Published by: Grapevine Books (Ediciones De La Parra)
Copyright © A. J. Parr 2014-2016. All Rights Reserved.

ISBN-13: 978-1532756016

ISBN-10: 1532756011

CONTENT

FOREWORD: FACING NEGATIVITY

Page 1

* * *

I: THE VALUE OF ADVERSITY
Exercise 1: Stopping your Thoughts

Page 9

* * *

II: WE ARE WHAT WE THINK
Exercise 2: Watching your Thoughts

Page 19

* * *

III: THE VOICE OF THE UNCONSCIOUS
Exercise 3: Breath Meditation

Page 31

* * *

IV: REPETITIVE NEGATIVE THINKING
Exercise 4: Feeling the Inner Body

Page 47

* * *

V: TRAPPED IN PAST AND FUTURE
Exercise 5: Feeling the Timeless Gap

Page 57

* * *

VI: NEGATIVITY AND RESISTANCE
Exercise 6: Surrendering to the Now

Page 71

* * *

VII: EXPERIENCING THE JOY OF LIVING
Exercise 7: Beating Negative Thinking

Page 81

* * *

ABOUT THE AUTHOR

Page 91

FOREWORD

FACING NEGATIVITY

"Whether we are happy in our individual or family life is, in a large part, up to us. Of course, material conditions are an important factor for happiness and a good life, but one's mental attitude is of equal or greater importance."

Dalai Lama

SCIENTISTS ESTIMATE THAT IN normal conditions a human being regularly has an average of 30,000 to 40,000 daily thoughts. This means that if most of our thoughts are pessimistic, we can actually end up having tens of thousands negative thoughts in just a single day!

According to research, *"depression is always preceded by repetitive negative thinking"* and not vice versa, and *"reducing the number of negative thoughts per day actually reduces both the frequency and intensity of depressive feelings and emotions"*!

These crucial findings constitute the starting point of the 7 Lessons and 7 Exercises contained in this beginner's guidebook, designed to help you break the habit of negative thinking by applying the teachings of Eckhart Tolle, who claims that:

> ****Most people ignore they are unceasingly generating negative thoughts and that they have the power to stop!***

> ****Most people do not realize that their depression, despair, rage, hopelessness and unhappiness are generated by their own repetitive negative-thinking.***

Most people believe that in order to stop their endless flow of pessimistic thoughts they first need to get rid of their negative feelings and emotions – but it is actually the other way around!

BREAKING OUR CHILDHOOD PATTERNS

According to research, we picked up most of the thinking patterns we repeat in the present back when we were only small children and didn't know better. Fact is, each time we felt threatened, abandoned, hurt or under attack as kids, we always *"reacted defensively"* by repeating the same specific patterns of thought and behavior– such as crying, fleeing, screaming, feeling guilty, hating, cursing, fearing, attacking, blaming others or yourself, or simply ignoring the world and sinking in our own thoughts!

Studies prove that the more a child repeats frequent negative thoughts like *"no one likes me"*, *"I hate my family"*, *"my parents don't love me"*, "I feel sad" or *"I'm an idiot"*, the unhappier he will feel and the longer it will affect him – even during the rest of his life!

They have also found that the child will develop an increasing number of "dysfunctional" patterns, sinking deeper and deeper in a sea of suffering and experiencing life-long consequences that lead to chronic depression, illness and, in some cases, even suicide!

Let's take a quick look, for example, at the celebrated case of 10-year-old Ulrich, who in spite of his young age, publicly admitted having had repetitive suicidal thoughts for years.

Ulrich was born in a dysfunctional family and admitted having a "miserable" childhood. He didn't like school because he had a hard time socializing and *the environment was so hostile.* And he didn't like his home either because his parents were always screaming, fighting and in the verge of divorce...

REPETITIVE THINKING PATTERNS

Young Ulrich grew up as an introverted lone wolf. In one of his many interviews he admits having had a *"deep intimacy with nature"*, in spite of the fact of growing up in a fairly big city.

He explained that one of the activities he most enjoyed was riding his bike after class and leaving behind what he called *"the miserable world of school"*. He would then ride beyond the outskirts of the city and rest in a solitary place all by himself, where he would admire *"the world of nature"* with a single repetitive thought running over and over through his head:

"This will always be here, this will always be here."

Ulrich admitted having his first suicidal thoughts in primary school. He acknowledged repeatedly hearing the same fatidic questions, over and over in his mind:

"How can I eliminate myself from this world?"

"How can I commit suicide?"

Repeating these suicidal thoughts over and over became a habit for young Ulrich - and later an addiction! But he had no choice. He simply couldn't stop repeating the same thoughts over and over!

It took Ulrich decades of inner struggle and suffering to finally break this addiction -we'll see how in the following pages. In sum, he survived all right, but unfortunately many kids who were his age were not so lucky:

> *A US study reveals that suicide is the fourth largest cause of mortality among children between the ages 10 and 14. And according to two Swiss surveys approximately 3% of the boys and 8% of the girls between the age of 11 and 15 admitted to having attempted against their lives at least once – even at the age of 7!*

ULRICH´S INNER STRUGGLE

Apart from suicidal thoughts that often came and went, Ulrich admitted that by the time he was ten he had already worked out several possibilities of how to kill himself.

During the years that followed, his suicidal urges persisted and he also experienced periods of intense depression. Finally, at the age of thirteen he refused to go to school any longer. He said it was too hostile and that he couldn´t take it anymore! So he did not receive any form of formal education all through his teens and not before becoming a grown adult, when he finally decided to continue studying and actually managed to obtain a university degree in London.

But even that didn't satisfy him! He continued experiencing constant depressions and didn't know how to stop the recurrent suicidal thinking pattern he had picked up as a child!

TURNING LEAD INTO GOLD

As the years passed, Ulrich invariably continued experiencing severe depressions and suicidal crisis. But finally, at the age of twenty-nine, he finally suffered the historic depression destined to forever transform his life.

Two things are for sure:

Ulrich never believed that one day he would break his suicidal thinking pattern literally overnight, like he did. And he never even imagined that he was destined to become one of the world's top authorities in the study of repetitive thoughts, mental patterns, suicidal tendencies, observing the mind, breaking the habit of negative thinking, experiencing inner stillness and enjoying the joy of Living and inner peace, rediscovering the basis of what he later defined as the ancient alchemic secret of the *"transmutation of base metal into gold, of suffering into consciousness!"*

And yes, in case you still haven't guessed it or have no idea, I am talking about the worldwide-famous spiritual guide and bestselling author ***Ulrich Leonard Tolle***, better known by his pen name ***Eckhart Tolle***, whose stands among the selected Great Masters consulted in this brief guidebook for beginners, humbly designed to help you begin to positively transform your life ***starting today***!

Let us rejoice and contemplate eternity!

Namaste!

I: THE VALUE OF ADVERSITY

"Due to the ignorance of the real nature of one's own being, which is happiness itself, people struggle in the vast ocean of material existence, forsaking the right path that leads to happiness..."

Ramana Maharshi

THE FIRST STEP OF STOPPING NEGATIVE THINKING consists in accepting that adversity is part of the natural *"ups and downs"* of life and that it actually hides *"priceless lessons"* that can boost our spiritual progress and inner growth. Unfortunately, most people do not understand this and are swept by the fierce waters of their own negativity.

In *"The Art of Happiness: A Handbook for Living"* (1998), the Dalai Lama states that *"the very purpose of our life is to seek (and attain) happiness"*. He adds that as human beings *"we all desire happiness and not to suffer"* and that *"each individual has a right to pursue happiness and avoid suffering"*.

But how can we truly attain happiness and end our suffering? Is this really possible?

To answer this question, as the Dalai Lama points out, above all we must understand that *"external circumstances are not what draw us into suffering"* and that *"suffering is caused and permitted by our own mind"*.

Truth is, what we call "negative events" in our lives are not necessarily negative for they can actually impel our spiritual progress and transformation. We just saw Eckhart Tolle´s case. He never have attained enlightenment had he not faced adversity in his childhood and youth

Eckhart admits that before turning thirty, back in his student days, he found himself continuously trapped in profound states of negative thinking that irremediably kept him *"deeply identified with thinking and the painful, heavy emotions accumulated within"*. Back then, his mind was constantly flooded with pessimistic thoughts and his general negativity grew day by day. And despite the fact that he experienced a brief periods of happiness and tranquility when he finished his studies and graduated, scarcely weeks later his *"unpleasant dream of thinking and painful emotions"* made their way back.

The return of this *"continuous anxiety interspersed with periods of suicidal depression"* soon triggered what Eckhart describes as a nightmarish state of depression and anxiety that literarily became unbearable. And that's when, as he acknowledged, one night he heard *"the voice in his head"* repeatedly declaring once and again:

"I cannot live with myself any longer."

"I cannot live with myself any longer."

"I cannot live with myself any longer."

This was the reiterative thought that kept repeating itself in his mind, over and over, the night he decided to end his life without suspecting that this nightmarish state would soon change his fate drastically – not only affecting his own life but millions around the globe!

WE CREATE OUR OWN HELL

What is "hell"? A subterranean realm filled with devils, flames and burning sinners or like most contemporary spiritual teachers claim, including pope Francis, only a state of mind?

Four-hundred years ago, the English poet John Milton (1608-1674) tackled this question after tragically losing his sight at the age of 44 – just when he was starting to gain literary fame! To make things worse, scarcely three months after going completely blind, his wife died and a few more later, their one-year-old son followed.

John Milton was left completely shattered!

Not only darkness was all he could see, but another type of darkness now fell upon him: the darkness of suffering and growing despair, comparable to Eckhart's *"continuous anxiety interspersed with periods of suicidal depression"*!

For less critical reasons many people have opted to take their own lives!

Driven by a lifelong quest for higher understanding, John Milton resisted what many would agree on calling *"real hell on*

12

earth". But instead of giving up on life, he turned his tragedy into a valuable source of lessons that led the way for the adoption of new "*patterns of thinking and behaving*". He thus learned to see his cup half-filled instead of half-empty, turning darkness into light.

Not only did Milton remarry and father more children but he also he hired a secretary, resumed his writing career and in fact dictated his literary masterpiece, "*Lost Paradise*" in spite of total blindness, literally "*making a heaven out of hell*".

In his own words, as Milton declared in his celebrated book:

> "*The mind is its own place and in itself can make a Heaven of Hell, a Hell of Heaven.*"

Regarding his personal tragedy and how he learned to cope with his loss of sight, he made the following confession in "*Lost Paradise*":

> "*To be blind is not miserable; not to be able to bear blindness, that is miserable.*"

As these pages explain in detail, the true source of pessimism is that most people do not know they are constantly "*making a hell out of heaven*" by continuously filling their heads with endless negative thoughts.

Why?

Because most people are continuously thinking about a *"better future"* or *"better past"* that only exist in their heads and which they nevertheless consider *"better than present reality"*, thus always leaving the *"real world"* in last place.

By continuously resisting and complaining, we unceasingly and indisputably believe *"we are better and worth more than this"* and that *"we deserve a better life"*.

In sum, by perpetually filling our minds with thoughts of a better *"future life"* we recurrently reject the present and perceive it as *"inferior"*, *"unsatisfactory"*, *"insufficient"*, *"incomplete"*, "undesirable." And even *"unbearable"*. And repeatedly doing this has become a negative and sometimes fatal habit we cannot break!

TURNING LEAD INTO GOLD

Alchemy has been historically known as the ancient and legendary art of turning lead into gold. In ancient times it was studied by most respected men of science and with the passing of the centuries became the mother of modern chemistry and pharmacology.

However, according to the Swiss psychoanalyst Carl Jung, the ancient art does not refer to real gold and metals, but to the transformation of the human soul by turning ignorance into knowledge, unconsciousness into consciousness...

And that's the secret of Alchemy, as we shall see in the following pages, the inner art of transmuting lead into gold, darkness into light, suffering into joy and, as John Milton claimed, hell into heaven!

EXERCISE 1: STOPPING YOUR THOUGHTS

The enquiry "Who am I?" is the principal means to the removal of all misery and the attainment of the supreme bliss. ...

Ramana Maharshi

IN THE MILLENARY INDIAN EPIC POEM known as the *Bhagavad Gita*, in which Lord Krishna and his dear disciple, prince Arjuna, discuss the difficulties of controlling the mind before the start of the legendary battle of *Kurukshetra*.

The ancient Hindu chronicle starts out when Arjuna tells Krishna he is full of doubts and cannot control his thoughts:

"Restless indeed is the mind!" **Arjuna finally exclaims.** *"It is vehement, strong and unconquerable. Controlling it seems to me as hard as trying to control the wind!"*

To this, Krishna replied with words of wisdom:

"You speak the truth, Arjuna. Without doubt, the mind is restless and very difficult to restrain. But I can assure you that the mind can be controlled by constant practice and non-attachment..."

STOPPING YOUR THINKING MIND

The following exercise consists in voluntarily stopping your thoughts at least for 20 seconds and see if you can.

To practice it, just follow these steps:

STEP 1:

Sit or lie down in a comfortable and relaxing position - the position you now have can do – and close your eyes before taking a deep breath to clear your mind.

Inhale… exhale…

STEP 2:

Mentally tell yourself that you will now stop thinking for at least 20 seconds just to prove you can and are in control.

STEP 3:

Mentally start counting from 1 to 20 and do your best not to have new thoughts. See how far you can go without having a single thought.

STEP 4:

While you count, one or more *"involuntary thoughts"* are bound to appear in your mind. Each time a new thought arises, stop counting.

Go back to the start and start counting from one all over again. So be alert, maintain a high level of inner awareness and stop every time a new thought arises.

For example:

> *"One, two, three, etc."where did I leave my keys?*
> *Ooops! One, two, three, etc." I'm doing better! Oh,*
> *no! One, two, three, etc."I'm hungry! For Christ's*
> *sake! One, two, three, etc."*

STEP 5:

If you can't do it the first time, repeat the process for at least three to five times. But don't worry, because if you fail to stop your thoughts, like most people, it does not mean you failed the exercise.

On the contrary, it means you succeeded, for this is what this practice is intended to prove (perhaps for the first time in your life) that you are not in complete control of your thoughts and that these can actually arise without your conscious awareness and control, as we will expand in the following lessons and exercises.

II: WE ARE WHAT WE THINK

"He who is enveloped by this veiling power (maya or illusion), wise or learned though he may be, clever, expert in the meaning of the scriptures, capable of wonderful achievements, will not be able to grasp the Truth..."

Ramana Maharshi

THE SECOND STEP OF STOPPING YOUR NEGATIVE THINKING consists in understanding that *"we are what we think"* and that we create our entire psychological reality based on a mental picture that only exists in our head!

To understand this we must first consider that one thing is *"the real world"* and another completely different is *"the idea we have of the real world"*.

The *"real world"* is the one and only reality or universal truth, while the second is nothing but a mental picture or *"illusory world"* that only exists in our heads!

Despite the fact that for centuries popular saying from all over the world have repeated more or less literally that *"every head is a world"* and that *"it all depends on the color of the glass you're looking through"*, most people have never stopped to think about the "real" implications of this.

It means that you and I, as well as everyone else on this planet have a double-perception of reality: one real and the other only a psychological illusion we blindly take for real! And this illusion is precisely the radical source of human suffering and all our negative thoughts and behaviors, including our self-inflicted feelings of sadness, loneliness, hatred, regret, dissatisfaction, greed, anger, envy, fear, remorse, impatience and evilness.

Instead of experiencing reality as it truly is, every one of us has created an illusory world in his or her own mind, a *"fictitious representation of the world"* that only exists in our own head, as explained in the following pages, a creation of our own minds molded by our thoughts, ideals, beliefs, values, judgments and fears, among others.

Truth is, for thousands of years the Hindus have spoken of this *"illusory world"* created by our own mind and traditionally known as the "veil" or "dream of maya".

This state of illusion makes us perceive reality not *"as it truly is"* but as *"we think it is"*, according to our own personal and particular interpretations. For example, I may think buying a new car will make me a happy person, but my next-door neighbor may not be interested in getting a new car and perhaps actually believes he'll only be happy if he wins a political election or divorces his wife.

In the same fashion, every one of us has created a personal interpretation of our reality and what we think we need, creating a definite gap between *"the way we perceive things"* and *"the way things truly are"*.

THE WORLD OF DELUSION

Most people spend their lives chasing success, fame, riches, power, pleasure, honor, social acceptance, excitement, respect and love, among other illusory dreams, hoping that these will one day grant them everlasting happiness and make their world a better place.

However, as the Hindu Sage Ramana Maharshi stated, these are vain pursuits for *"the world should be considered like a dream."*

But why? Simply because each one of us, instead of experiencing reality as it truly is, have created an illusory world, a *"fictitious representation of the world"* that only exists within our own mind.

This *"fictitious representation of the world"*, as we shall see in the following pages, is the creation of our own minds and is molded by our thoughts, ideals, beliefs, values, judgments and fears, among others.

Truth is, for thousands of years the Hindus have spoken of this *"illusory world"* created by our own mind and traditionally known as the "veil" or "dream of maya".

As Ramana Maharshi explained:

"Maya is that which makes us regard as non-existent the Self, the Reality, which is always and everywhere present, all-pervasive and self-luminous…"

This state of illusion makes us perceive reality not *"as it truly is"* but as *"we think it is"*, according to our own personal and particular interpretations. For example, I may think buying a new car will make me a happy person, but my next-door neighbor may not be interested in getting a new car and perhaps actually believes he'll only be happy if he gets a new job or divorces his wife.

In the same fashion, every one of us has created a personal interpretation of our own reality and what we think we need, creating a definite gap between *"the way we think things are or should be"* and *"the way things truly are"*.

Unfortunately, this mental perception of the world produces a *"distorted view of reality"*, generated and sustained by our own thoughts, especially by all the negative thoughts we constantly repeat, according to the following psychological principle:

> *"The more we repeat a specific thought about the world or ourselves, the more it affects our perception of the world and our self-image."*

Positive repetitive thoughts generate positive emotions when we think about them. But in the case of negative repetitive thoughts these produce anxiety, depression, dissatisfaction, rage, chronic stress as well as physical and mental disorders.

WE ARE WHAT WE THINK

According to the ancient legend, around 2,500 years ago the Buddha was the first to publicly proclaim that:

"We are what we think. All that we are arises with our thoughts and with our thoughts we make... "

Regarding this, the *Dvedhavitakka Sutta* gives us the following explanation:

"Whatever a monk pursues by thinking and considering, disposes his awareness.

"If a monk pursues thinking filled with sensuality, leaving behind thinking filled with renunciation, his mind will be bent by that thinking filled with sensuality.

"If a monk continuously pursues thinking filled with ill will, leaving behind thinking filled with non-ill will, his mind will be bent by that thinking filled with ill will.

"If a monk continuously pursues thinking filled with harmfulness, leaving behind thinking filled with harmlessness,

his mind will be bent by that thinking filled with harmfulness."

MADE BY THOUGHTS

Over two thousand years ago the celebrated Greek philosopher Epictetus (55-135 AD) stated:

"People are not disturbed by things, but by the view they take of them."

Similarly, the Roman leader Marcus Antonius (83-30 BC) conveyed this fact in his own words:

"Consider how much more you often suffer from your anger and grief, than from those very things for which you are angry and grieved."

In his own words, the Roman emperor and philosopher Marcus Aurelius Antoninus (121-180 AD) in his celebrated *"Meditations"* sustained:

"Our life is what our thoughts make it... If you are distressed by something external, the pain is not due to the thing itself but to your own opinion about it and thus you have the power to revoke it at

any moment... All we hear is just an opinion, not a fact. All we see is a perspective, not real truth."

Regarding this truth, the nineteenth-century American psychologist and philosopher William James (1842-1910) noted that *"man can alter his life by altering his thinking"*, adding that:

"Whilst part of what we perceive comes through our senses from the objects around us, another part (perhaps the larger) comes always from our own head."

Last but not least, the same truth was expressed by the British philosopher James Allen (1864-1912) in his bestselling book *"As Man Thinketh"*, in which he claimed that we are *"made and unmade"* by our own thoughts:

"Man is made or unmade by himself; in the armory of thought he forges the weapons by which he destroys himself; he also fashions the tools with which he builds for himself heavenly mansions of joy and strength and peace."

EXERCISE 2: WATCHING YOUR THOUGHTS

"You have probably come across 'mad' people in the street incessantly talking or muttering to themselves. Well, that's not much different from what you and all other 'normal' people do, except that you don't do it out loud. The voice comments, speculates, judges, compares, complains, likes, dislikes, and so on."

Eckhart Tolle

THE FOLLOWING BEGINNING EXERCISE will allow you to observe our thoughts as they arise and begin to experience your first *"gaps of inner stillness"*, as Eckhart Tolle explains:

> **"Start listening to the voice in your head as often as you can. This is what I mean by 'watching the thinker,' which is another way of saying: 'Listen to the voice in your head, be there as the witnessing presence.'"**

According to the nineteenth century Hindu monk Swami Vivekananda (1863-1902) unless we learn to tame our mind it will continuously jump around like a *"wild monkey"*, forever swinging from branch to branch and jumping from thought to thought:

> *"How hard it is to control the mind! It has been well compared with the maddened monkey."*

Vivekananda recommended silently observing the mind and being aware of it *"bubbling up all the time"*:

> *"It is like that monkey jumping about. Let the monkey jump as much as he can; you simply wait and watch."*

WATCHING YOUR THOUGHTS

To do this exercise, just follow these steps:

FIRST:

Sit or lie down in a comfortable and relaxing position. The position you now have while reading this book will do.

SECOND:

Close your eyes. Although you can also do this exercise with your eyes open, I recommend doing it with your eyes closed this first time to avoid unwanted distractions and increase your inner concentration.

Now say to yourself:

> *"'I wonder what my next thought is going to be.' Then become very alert and wait for the next thought. Be like a cat watching a mouse hole. What thought is going to come out of the mouse hole? Try it now."*

THIRD:

Soon a new thought will appear in your head, for example: *"I'm thirsty"* or *"I'm having a thought"*.

FOURTH:

Whatever you do, first recognize that you are having a thought and then observe it without judging it or starting an inner conversation before letting it go and focusing your attention back to your inner state of alertness and silently wait for your next thought.

"Be like a cat watching a mouse hole."

FIFTH:

Repeat the process several times for one or two minutes, avoiding to engage in *"inner chat"* at all cost. Practicing this exercise, as we shall see in the following pages, will be most useful whenever you choose to make your repetitive negative thoughts lose their power over you, as *The Power of Now* indicates:

> *"As you listen to the thought, you feel a conscious presence - your deeper self - behind or underneath the thought, as it were. The thought then loses its power over you and quickly subsides, because you are no longer energizing the mind through identification with it."*

III: THE VOICE OF THE UNCONSCIOUS

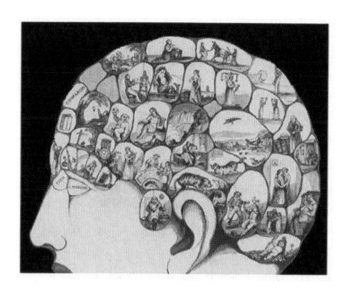

"Maya is that which makes us regard as non-existent the Self, the Reality, which is always and everywhere present, all-pervasive and self-luminous..."

Ramana Maharshi

THE THIRD STEP OF STOPPING YOUR NEGATIVE THINKING consists in recognizing that all our thoughts are only words, symbols and mental pictures comparable to the words, symbols and pictures or personal computer.

Human thinking, as we all know, is fundamentally based on "words", which also constitute the basis of oral speech and written communication. However, words are only symbols.

But most people forget this.

The word "moon" for example, is used to represent the real moon. But it is not the actual moon. In fact, someone who has never seen the moon or its picture cannot "imagine" the real moon unless he actually sees it. In any other case, his mental representation of the moon will necessarily be inaccurate, false.

Likewise, when we speak of "Truth" or "Illusion" there is no way you can truly understand their meaning unless you actually experience these.

It is said that the Buddha warned his followers not to try to rationally understand his teachings or to stick to his words but to try to see beyond instead:

"My teaching is like a finger pointing to the moon. Do not mistake the finger for the moon."

As this simile states, "transcendental truth" cannot be expressed with words. Anything you believe or say about it is only "a finger pointing to the moon".

And since all words are merely "fingers pointing to the moon", we must be careful about what they mean.

Don't be a fool, the Buddha states, the description of reality is not reality... The finger is not the point...: the point is the moon!

Therefore, don't fall into the senseless trap of believing that your personal interpretation of reality and Truth is the absolutely reliable.

In order to understand the worthlessness of using words or reasoning when trying to communicate a direct experience try answering the following question:

Can you describe the flavor of chocolate to someone who has never tasted it?

It seems rather hard, doesn't it?

Honestly, I find it totally impossible. No matter which words you use, your description will always be inaccurate and can never transmit what you are really trying to express: the flavor of chocolate to someone who has never tasted it.

In sum, the only way to understand what the flavor of chocolate is all about is by experiencing it, that is, by tasting it (direct experience).

33

Like the celebrated martial arts master and movie star Bruce Lee once said, paraphrasing the Budhha:

"Be like a finger pointing at the moon, but do not focus on the finger or you will miss all the heavenly glory."

THE PARABLE OF THE ARROW

According to Buddha, spiritual understanding can only be attained through direct experience and not through reasoning. In fact, trying to understand his teachings intellectually is actually an obstacle when trying to free yourself from the chains of illusion.

Similarly, freeing ourselves from the chains of illusion and attaining liberation cannot be described with words. It can only be understood by direct experience.

And that's what this book is all about: Finding inner peace, everlasting happiness and self-knowledge is not a matter of using words and symbols but a matter of direct experience, as the following pages evidence.

OUR ENDLESS MENTAL CHATTER

Words are the essence of our endless mental chatter. This is why the Indian philosopher Jiddu Krisnamurti (1895-1986) usually referred to the thinking mind as the *"chattering mind"*, stating that this chatter is a constant process, an endless operation, and that *"every moment it is murmuring"*.

In his 1954 best-seller *"The First and Last Freedom"* he stated:

> *"As I watch the brain, I see that the chattering happens only in the brain, it is a brain activity; a current flows up and down, but it is chaotic, meaningless and purposeless. The brain wears itself out by its own activity. One can see that it is tiring to the brain, but it does not stop... The mind chatters all the time and the energy devoted to that purpose fills a major part of our life.*
>
> *"The mind apparently needs to be occupied with something... The mind is occupied with something and if it is not occupied, it feels vacant, it feels empty and therefore it resorts to chattering..."*

THE VOICE IN THE HEAD

The source of our mental chatter is what Eckhart Tolle calls *"the voice in the head"*, which is seemingly produced in the hidden depths of our mind and hurled into the conscious levels without our voluntary control. Although this voice continuously comments, complains, guesses, judges, compares, approves and disapproves seemingly on its own, each thought is only the end result of a continuous and strictly automatic process based on the impulsive repetition of what he calls *"unconscious mental-emotional reactive patterns"*.

Truth is, our repetitive negative thoughts are only *"reflexive reactions"* based on unconscious patterns of behavior conditioned by repetition, such as the act of continuously reviving a recent or distant undesirable past and thus causing self-inflicted suffering, sadness, regret, remorse, hatred or guilt or, on the other hand, the act of continuously imagining a possible negative situation in the future, often expecting things to go wrong and fearing a negative outcome thus causing self-inflicted pain, tension, worry, anxiety, fear, rage, stress and unhappiness, among other reflexive responses.

THE ROLE OF THE UNCONSCIOUS

The Father of Psychoanalysis, the Viennese neurologist Sigmund Freud based his revolutionary psychological theory on the fact that the human mind operates in two basic levels or layers: One is superficial, known as the "conscious", while the other lies hidden in the deepest layers of our minds, known as the "unconscious".

This dual nature of the mind is commonly explained by the *"iceberg metaphor"*, which states that the conscious is only the tip of the iceberg and that the enormous and unseen unconscious perennially hide beneath the surface.

36

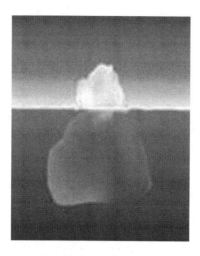

Just like a floating iceberg –or ice-cube for that matter–it mostly sinks in water with only a small part surfacing, which represents our conscious, which only constitutes a small part of our whole mind.

Freud was the first to announce that the workings of our thinking mind mostly take place in the deep and hidden layers of the unconscious – totally without our conscious awareness! He was also the first to compare the unconscious with a vast "storage-room" ("memory unit") where we keep all the information we have gathered and processed ever since we were born ("data"), including unconscious repetitive reactions based inner impulses.

According to him, our unconscious actually runs and controls our thinking mind and based on this he defined analytical therapy as the way of inducing mental sanity by *turning unconscious processes into conscious awareness*.

THE MASTER OF YOUR MIND

In his *"Introduction to Psychoanalysis"*, Freud concludes what most people do not accept that the 'I' is not a *"master in its own home"* and that in reality we are governed by *"all that goes on unconsciously"*:

> **"In the course of time humanity has had to withstand two great indignations against its naive self-love from the hands of science.**

> **"The first took place when humans first discovered that our planet is not the center of this universe, but only a minute speck in a world-system hardly imaginable in its enormousness. We associate this with Copernicus, though Alexandrian scientists had already taught more or less the same.**

> **"The second took place when biological research robbed man of his alleged superiority and special creation, proving his descent from the animal kingdom and everlasting animal nature. This new vision, presented by Charles**

Darwin, Wallace and their predecessors, was not accepted without the most aggressive antagonism of their contemporaries.

"Nevertheless, the third and most irritating offence is presently being thrown against the human mania of greatness by psychological research, which is set to prove to the 'I' that it is not even master in its own home, but dependent on the scantiest information concerning all that goes on unconsciously in its psychic life."

"We psychoanalysts are not the first nor the only ones to announce the admonition to look within ourselves. It seems that we are destined to insistently prove this most insistently and confirm it by means of empirical data which to all individuals are of importance..."

OUR UNCONSCIOUS ASSUMPTIONS

According to Eckhart Tolle, the thinking mind is continuously processing thoughts and emotions in its deepest layers, generating all sorts of negative thoughts and reactive behaviors that continuously disturb us, based on by what he calls our *"unconscious assumptions"*:

> ***"'People cannot be trusted' would be an example of an unconscious assumption in a person whose primordial relationships, that is to say, parents or siblings, were not supportive and did not inspire trust."***

Psychologists have long found that the constant repetition of specific thoughts can actually "program" our minds–both positively and negatively–and that in fact these can *"distort our perception of reality"*, thus modifying our self-image and general state of wellbeing.

The influence of these repetitive thoughts were first studied by the American psychologist Albert Ellis, the second most influential psychologist of all times according to the American Psychological Association (APA), who in the mid-1950's based his Rational Emotive Behavior Therapy (REBT) on the premise that *"we largely feel according to the way we think"*.

According to Ellis, people are influenced not by negative events but by their *"catastrophic"* repetitive thoughts and beliefs about these events. And these are always based on what he called *"irrational assumptions about what we must be and do"*.

Among others, Eckhart mentions the following common *"unconscious assumptions"* in *The Power of Now*:

'Nobody respects or appreciates me'

'I need to struggle for survival

'I never have enough money'

'Life always lets me down'

'I don't deserve abundance'.

'I don't deserve love'

According to him, repeating these assumptions constantly transform or distort our personal reality without our awareness:

> *"Unconscious assumptions create emotions in the body which in turn generate mind activity and/or instant reactions. This way they create your personal reality...*

> **"The ego is not only the unobserved mind, 'the voice in the head' which**

41

pretends to be you, but also the unobserved emotions that are the body's reaction to what the voice in the head is saying. We have already seen what kind of thinking the egoic voice engages in most of the time and the dysfunction inherent in the structure of its thought processes, regardless of content.

"Dysfunctional thinking is what the body reacts to with negative emotion: The voice in the head tells a story that the body believes in and reacts to. Those reactions are the emotions. The emotions, in turn, feed energy back to the thoughts that created the emotion in the first place.

"Such is the vicious circle between our unexamined thoughts and emotions, thus giving rise to emotional thinking and emotional story-making. The emotional component of ego differs from person to person. In some egos, it is greater than in others..."

EXERCISE 3: BREATH MEDITATION

"Meditation is never the control of the body. There is no actual division between the organism and the mind. The brain, the nervous system and the thing we call the mind are one, indivisible. It is the natural act of meditation that brings about the harmonious movement of the whole. To divide the body from the mind and to control the body with intellectual decisions is to bring about contradiction, from which arise various forms of struggle, conflict and resistance..."

Krishnamurti

BREATH MEDITATION IS A HELPFUL PRACTICE based on becoming aware of our breath as it moves in and out of our body. Eckhart Tolle sustains in *A New Earth* that a single deep breath taken consciously, can slow down your thoughts and end your "inner chatter":

> ***"One conscious breath is enough to make some space where before there was the uninterrupted succession of one***

thought after another. One conscious breath (two or three would be even better), taken many times a day, is an excellent way of bringing space into your life.

BASIC STEPS OF THIS PRACTICE

Although the practice of breathing meditation or breath awareness has many different variations, all of them are based on consciously following *"the flow of your breath"*:

FIRST:

You can do this simple practice in any position you like: sitting, laying down, standing or in any position adopt while doing you regular daily routines, such as driving, walking, riding a vehicle or elevator, waiting on line or for an appointment, rushing up and down the steps at home or work, riding a bicycle, jogging, listening to music, washing your hands, bathing or simply while placidly resting in a park or beach.

SECOND:

Consciously take a few deep breaths concentrating on each time you inhale and exhale, following Eckhart's basic guidelines:

"Don't try judge or control your breath – realize that breathing isn't something you do but something you witness or observe. Breathing is autonomous and effortless. Your unconscious inner intelligence is in charge of it. Be the silent Witness, breathe and observe!"

"Even if you meditate on your breath for 2 hours or more - which some people do – a single breath is all you ever need to be aware of, indeed ever can be aware of. The rest is only memory or anticipation, that is to say, only thought."

THIRD:

Continue focused on each breath and whenever a new thought arises, simply be aware of it without getting "hooked" and let it go before turning your attention back to the physical sensation of *"your abdomen expanding and contracting slightly with each inhalation and exhalation"*.

FOURTH:

Keep your attention focused on breathing consciously and repeat the process each time a new thought arises, until your flow of thoughts gradually slow down and you start to experience the silent gaps of inner stillness between thoughts (or between breaths), as detailed in *The Power of Now,* without ceasing to consciously:

> *"Feel yourself breathing into the lower abdomen and observe how it slightly expands and contracts with each in and out breath…"*

5: A more "visual" practice recommended by Eckhart consists in closing your eyes and consciously breathing while picturing yourself surrounded by a bright light or immersed in a luminous sea of consciousness before imagining yourself breathing or sinking in that light and starting to glow with intense brightness, as *The Power of Now* also instructs:

> *"Then gradually focus more on the feeling. Don't get attached to visual images. You are now in your body. You have accessed the power of Now."*

IV: REPETITIVE NEGATIVE THINKING

"The brain wears itself out by its own activity. One can see that it is tiring to the brain, but it does not stop… The mind chatters all the time and the energy devoted to that purpose fills a major part of our life."

Krishnamurti

THE INFLUENCE OF OUR REPETITIVE NEGATIVE THOUGHTS and how they actually alter or distort our perception of the world and of ourselves was first studied in the 1960s by the American psychiatrist and University of Pennsylvania professor Aaron T. Beck, better known as the Father of Cognitive Therapy.

Beck gave these altered perceptions the name of *"cognitive distortions"* and concluded they are exclusively sustained by the regular repetition of common negative thoughts such as:

"I feel so lonely!"

"I will never be happy".

"I need to be accepted."

"People always take advantage of me."

"I always have bad luck."

"I feel so depressed!"

"I cannot do anything right!"

"I will never succeed!"

"I will never be happy!"

"Nobody cares about me!"

"No one will ever love me!"

"No one understands me!

"Nobody can be trusted."

"I'm truly unattractive or ugly."

"I'm a loser!"

"He or she does not like or accept me."

"I'm so stupid!"

"I hate myself!"

"I can't stand it!"

THE TWO SIDES OF THE COIN

To understand how repetitive thinking affect us let's imagine the following example: Suppose an important bank hires a couple of young executives, both fresh out of college: the twin brothers Bill and Joe Smith.

The twins not only look exactly alike but also have the same physical and mental conditions and potentials. Their only big difference, however, lies in the nature of their thoughts:

Let's start with Bill. Unlike his brother he is always repeating to himself positive or optimistic thoughts like:

"I'm so glad I'm alive"

"I'm so happy"

"I have and important purpose in live"

"No pain no gain"

"People always like me"

"Each time I fail I am one step closer to success"

On the other hand, although both of them grew up with the same parents, his brother Joe somehow ended up being a pessimist and is always repeating to himself negative thoughts like:

"I hate my life"

"I can't do it"

"Nobody will ever love me"

"I'll never be happy"

And so, while Bill always sees a half-full glass, Joe always sees it half empty.

Fact is, Bill sees a world of opportunities and success, whereas Joe only sees a world of failure and sadness.

Which of the two do you think is more likely to succeed in life? And who seems more likely to fail and suffer?

TWO DIFFERENT WORLDS

As we have seen, Bill and Joe actually live in two different worlds in spite of their similar conditions and have very different perceptions of themselves.

Due to Joe´s negative thoughts, he perceives himself as a potential failure, unable to reach success, while Bill perceives himself as a successful man willing to overcome problems and work his way to success.

Both brothers have fabricated a mental image of themselves, each based on personal ideas and imagination: one is optimistic and the other pessimistic. But the fact that both these images were imaginary does not stop them from producing "real" consequences in their psyches.

Joe is possessed by his own pessimism, and his repetitive negative thoughts only sink him deeper and deeper in his dream of illusion. He represents the state of mind maintained by most people in the world, who unconsciously repeat negative thoughts without analyzing their origin or knowing how these can disturb them.

Joe´s dream of himself undoubtedly affects him deeply, creating self-inflicted suffering, insecurity, despair, rage, fear, and depression, among other consequences. He obviously perceives that *"something is always missing in life"* and feels *"incomplete"*. Because of this he always tries to find happiness in exterior objects, pleasures or people, believing that one day he will satisfy his most-esteemed desires and experience everlasting happiness and peace of mind.

What's Joe's biggest mistake?

Not realizing that he is only imagining things!

In reality, Joe has the same conditions and chances of succeeding as his brother. In fact, he has all he needs to experience true happiness here and now. But ignoring this truth constitutes his main problem.

Unfortunately most of us are just like Joe.

Influenced by our repetitive negative thoughts, we too have created a false perception of the world and of ourselves. And the more we think about and believe in these false perceptions, the more they will end up affecting us with negative emotions, as Eckhart explains:

"Almost every human body is under a great deal of strain and stress, not because it is threatened by some external factor but from within the mind."

EXERCISE 4: FEELING THE INNER BODY

"What I call the "inner body" isn't really the body anymore but life energy, the bridge between form and formlessness. Make it a habit to feel the inner body as often as you can."

Eckhart Tolle

ECKHART TOLLE RECOMMENDS stopping our endless flow of thoughts by experiencing what he calls our *"inner body"*. According to him, this is a fast and sure way of connecting with the Now by slowing down our thoughts and our *"mind chatter"*. And learning to do this at will is precisely what this exercise is all about!

According to Eckhart, to experience your inner body you must keep in mind a couple of basic principles:

*The body is a vehicle for experiencing Presence.

*You cannot experience Presence through your thoughts.

To practice this exercise follow these steps, as Eckhart indicates:

FIRST:

Close your eyes. Now concentrate on *"feeling"* your right hand without moving it.

Where is it? How can you know if it´s there? Instead of moving it, concentrate on *"feeling"* its aliveness. Do it now!

If you do this for several seconds, you will start to experience a slight *"inner tingling"* or *"inner warmth"* in your hand. Eckhart calls it *"your inner sense of aliveness"*, *"inner presence"* or *"being-ness"*.

Concentrate. Feel it. Experience it.

SECOND:

As you continue feeling this inner *"tingling"* or *"warmth"* in your hand, be observant and wait for your next thought.

"Be like a cat watching a mouse hole."

THIRD:

Each time a new thought arises, observe it, avoid judging or starting an inner conversation. Then simply let it go and bring back your attention to the feeling of inner aliveness within your hand.

FOURTH:

Although Eckhart recommends focusing on the hands, it really doesn't matter which part of your body you focus on. What's important is that you take your focus away from your thoughts and concentrate on something physical.

Now also direct your attention to your other hand and silently concentrate on feeling the aliveness within.

Can you feel it?

Gradually include the rest of your, beginning with your arms and slowly including your feet, your legs, your trunk and your head.

FIFTH:

Silently concentrate on the subtle energy field pervading your entire body. Feel it in all parts of your body simultaneously, as a single field of energy.

Don't think about it. Just feel it!

This is what Eckhart calls *"inner-body awareness"*. According to him, and as I have experienced countless times, the more you practice this form of meditation, the clearer and stronger your experience will get:

"You may get an image of your body becoming luminous. Although such an image can help you temporarily, pay more attention to the feeling than to any image that may arise. An image, no matter how beautiful or powerful, is already defined in form, so there is less scope for penetrating more deeply."

SIXTH:

Repeat this practice as often as you can for several days (at least a minute each time). You can do this at work or home, while driving, walking, jogging, riding the elevator, waiting on line or simply relaxing, among others.

The more you practice the more you will get in touch with what Eckhart calls your *"inner sense of aliveness"*, allowing you to temporarily leave all your thoughts and worries behind and start to gradually intensify the joyful feeling of experiencing the *Now*!

V: TRAPPED IN PAST AND FUTURE

"One does not become a king by merely saying, 'I am a king', without destroying one's enemies and obtaining the reality of power. Similarly, one does not obtain liberation... without destroying the duality caused by ignorance and directly experiencing the Self."

Ramana Maharshi

THE FOURTH STEP OF STOPPING YOUR NEGATIVE THINKING consists in learning to avoid getting *"stuck in time"* and thus escape from the traps of our past and future, which always sinks us in pessimism and distorts our view of reality.

Regarding the fact of being *"stuck in time"* and its negative consequences, over half a century ago the outstanding American writer Helen Keller (1880-1968), who went deaf and blind when she was only an infant and nevertheless reached world-wide fame as a prominent author and social activist expressed:

> *"When one door of happiness closes,*
> *another opens; but often we look so long*
> *at the closed door that we do not see the*
> *one which has been opened for us…"*

THE HABIT OF EVADING REALITY

By thinking continuously in our past (as well as in our future) we constantly evade reality. And by doing this we automatically neglect the present moment and always end up rejecting and even despising it!

Like most contemporary humans, we first adopted the habit of evading reality through constantly thinking when we were small children and have repeated this same pattern each time we have felt unsatisfied with the present moment for some reason or another.

In countless cases we have "compensated" our in satisfaction by losing ourselves in our own thoughts, imagining better times or remembering a longed-for past. And this precisely makes us neglect and resist to "what is".

A person with predominantly negative thoughts, as Eckhart Tolle points out, reflects an unevolved mind, that is, a primitive state of consciousness characterized by ignorance.

Since ancient times this *"untrained state of awareness"* has been compared with being *"asleep"*, *"blind"*, *"dreaming"*, *"unconscious"*, *"ignorant"* or *"in darkness"*."

Truth is we are all blind to certain degree. And as metaphorically described by John Milton, unless we awaken and accept "reality as it is" without resisting, we will always turn heaven into hell, as Eckhart Tolle suggests in *The Power of Now*:

"If you found yourself in paradise, it wouldn't be long before your mind would say 'yes, but...'"

THE DISEASE OF PSYCHOLOGICAL TIME

In 1968 Krishnamurti expressed the following during a series of talks he delivered in Puerto Rico:

"Psychological time only exists when there is comparison, when there is a distance to be covered between 'what is' and 'what should be', which is the desire to become somebody or nobody, all that involves psychological time and the distance to be covered."

To avoid negative thoughts and feelings he gave the following recommendation:

"When you have some experience of joy, of pleasure or whatever it is, live it completely and do not demand that it should endure, because then you are caught in time."

POSTPONING HAPPINESS

Most humans are always postponing their own happiness for they believe they do not deserve it and that they will only be happy sometime in the future. But only if they reach certain goal, become rich, buy a new car or home, get a juicy raise or a better job, get married or start a romantic relationship, win the lottery, or satisfy this or that other craving. As Carl Jung explains in the introduction of Heinrich Zimmer's *"The Way to the Self"*:

"Once he launches himself in pursuit of external things, man is never satisfied,

as evidenced when dealing with our bare necessities. He is always in pursuit of more and more and, true to his own prejudices, he always looks for that more in external things.

"He forgets completely that, in spite of all the external success, he remains the same inside, and thus complains about his poverty if he just owns a single car instead of two, like his neighbors. Undoubtedly, providing ourselves with everything that is necessary is a source of happiness that we should not underestimate.

"But above all, and transcending it, the inner man cries out that no external good can satisfy us; and the less attention is paid to this voice, in the middle of the hunt for the "wonderful things" of this world, the more the inner man creates an inexplicable source of bad luck and incomprehensible sorrow, while living a life of living conditions we could expect to produce something very different.

CRAVING FOR TOMORROW

Continuously craving for a *"better future"* automatically degrades our perception of the real world and the Now. Comparing the present moment with better times always makes it seem inferior and less desirable. This is why Eckhart Tolle explains that the road to awakening lies beyond judgments and comparisons. It consists in concentrating on being Present and on connecting yourself to the endless and ever generous flow of *"what is"*:

> **"All cravings are the mind seeking salvation or fulfillment in external things and in the future as a substitute for the joy of Being."**

MANAGING GOALS AND DESIRES

No matter what you expect to gain from these teachings, there is no need to give up your desires or stop working to fulfill them.

If the future and all we think about it is only an illusion, then what should we do? Does it mean we should completely stop thinking about tomorrow, avoid desiring things and forget all impending plans?

Not at all!

62

It only means, as we will see in the following pages, that above all you need to pursue your goals without overvaluation and overexcitement, recognizing the difference between clock time and psychological time and always keeping in mind that you do not depend on the future to experience the joy of Being here and now:

"If you set yourself a goal and work toward it, you are using clock time. You are aware of where you want to go, but you honor and give your fullest attention to the step that you are taking at this moment.

"If then you become excessively focused on the goal, perhaps because you seek happiness, fulfillment or a more complete sense of self, the Now is no longer honored. It becomes reduced to a mere stepping stone to the future without intrinsic value.

"Clock time then turns into "psychological time". Your life's journey no longer is an adventure, only an obsessive need to arrive, to attain, to 'make it.'

A. J.   P A R R

"You no longer see or smell the flowers by the wayside either. Nor are aware of the beauty and the miracle of life unfolding around you when you are present in the Now."

EXERCISE 5: THE TIMELESS GAP

"If you no longer want to create pain for yourself and others, if you no longer want to add to the residue of past pain that still lives on in you, then don't create any more time, or at least no more than is necessary to deal with the practical aspects of your life..."

Eckhart Tolle

TWO OF ECKHART TOLLE'S MAIN BASIC PRINCIPLES are that *"time and mind are inseparable"* and that *"remove time from the mind and it stops - unless you choose to use it!"*

But how on earth can we actually remove time from the mind?

Is this even possible?

Yes, according to Eckhart, who claims that doing this is relatively simple with some practice: All it takes is learning to *"read between the lines"* and experience the *"silent gap"* between thoughts. To understand and personally experience this, just follow these steps:

FIRST:

Observe your thoughts as most as you can during your daily routine. Identify your most frequent *"repetitive negative thoughts"* and write them down. This list will help you detect the thoughts you need to avoid.

Is there a predominant and repetitive thought present in your daily thinking? What is it? Is it directly or indirectly related with your present unhappiness?

SECOND:

Each time you find yourself repeating a same negative thought or thoughts over and over in your mind or engaged in *"negative mental chatter"*, remember it is you *"voice in the head"* repeating the same *"negative thinking pattern"* you have repeated for years (probably since you were a kid).

Realize it is not you who is doing the actual thinking and that your repetitive inner thoughts are only *"conditioned responses"* or *"reflexive reactions"* produced by your ego or *"thinking mind"*.

THIRD:

Next, immediately recognize that you are the owner of your mind and therefore always have the right to join or not in a mental conversation with your *"voice in the head"*. You both have and deserve that right – yours is the right to choose!

FOURTH:

Momentarily stop judging your own thoughts and avoid talking back or starting all inner dialogue. Now that you know better, don´t fall into the trap and consciously give it a no and refuse to participate.

To help you do this just follow the next step:

FIFTH:

As you continue observing your thoughts, now concentrate on the "silent gap between one and the next. These gaps of complete silence are *"glimpses of inner stillness"* and within them there is no thinking. Hence, no future nor past! Just a non-verbal consciousness of "Being" or "Presence", as Eckhart calls it.

The world´s main spiritual teachings mention the supreme importance of these silent gaps of inner stillness. They are also known as the "sound" or "voice" of *silence"*. Among these teachings, Eckhart includes those of Krishna, Buddha, Jesus, Rumi, Lao-Tze, Meister Eckhart, Ramana Maharshi, Krishnamurti, and *A Course In Miracles.*

SIXTH:

Concentrate on the silent gap for a few seconds. Simply concentrate on the total silence between one thought and the next. Be cautious for this silence may only last a brief instant, as mentioned in *Stillness Speaks*:

> *"Pay attention to the gap, the gap between two thoughts, the brief, silent space between words in a conversation, between the notes of a piano or flute, or the gap between the in-breath and the out-breath. When you pay attention to those gaps, awareness of 'something' becomes just awareness. The formless dimension of pure consciousness arises from within you and replaces identification with form."*

What does it feel like? You have a thought here, a thought there, and between each there's a little space, a blank or silent gap. Initially the experience may only last a second or even brief microseconds, so please pay close attention.

How long should the gaps ideally be? Don't worry about it! As Eckhart explains in *A New Earth:*

> *"You need not be concerned with the duration of those gaps. A few seconds is good enough. These will gradually*

lengthen themselves without effort on your behalf. More important than their length is bringing them in frequently so that your daily activities and stream of thinking become interspersed with space."

Eckhart describer that initially these silent gaps will be brief, only a few seconds perhaps. Nevertheless, with practice they will gradually become longer:

SEVENTH:

Repeat this exercise several times a day, preferably combining it with breath or inner body meditation, until managing to gradually experience longer gaps.

Each time a new thought arises, repeat the same process: Don´t judge it. Don´t engage in *"mental chatter"*. Just observe it, release it and then concentrate once more on experiencing the *"timeless gap between thoughts."*

By doing this, you will actually slow down and even stop your usual stream of thoughts and cease comparing the present moment with an imaginary *"before or after"*.

And thus, you will truly begin to free yourself from the trap of psychological time and the human compulsion of *"endless preoccupation with past and future and an unwillingness to honor and acknowledge the present moment and allow it to be":*

> **"The compulsion arises because the past gives you an identity and the future holds the promise of salvation, of fulfillment in whatever form. Both are illusions."**

VI: NEGATIVITY AND RESISTANCE

"While dreaming, all kinds of things may come to mind, but these are nothing more than appearances. Likewise, a magician may create a variety of illusory appearances, but they do not exist objectively..."

Dalai Lama

THE SIXTH STEP OF STOPPING NEGATIVE THINKING consists in learning to surrender without resistance to the endless flow "what it", as Eckhart Tolle describes in *The Power of Now*:

> *"Surrender is the simple but profound wisdom of yielding to rather than opposing the flow of life... The only place where you can experience the flow of life is the Now."*

What does Eckhart mean?

That we need to accept the present moment unconditionally ("Thy Will Be Done"); relinquishing all inner resistance to *"what is"*:

THE NEED TO SURRENDER

To avoid negativity and experience inner joy you must first learn to surrender. However, this does not mean *"throwing the towel"* or *"giving up on life"* as Eckhart explains:

> *"Surrender is perfectly compatible with taking action, initiating change or achieving goals. But in the surrendered state a totally different energy, a different quality, flows into your doing."*

72

Surrender means recognizing the illusory nature of our thoughts and desires; it means accepting things as they truly are and not as we imagine them to be. It means yielding to unexpected changes in life rather than opposing and resisting to them.

It means unconditionally accepting the present moment and what is real "here and now".

It also means accepting reality as it is by ceasing to compare it with ideal future or past realities that only exist in your head.

So give up waiting as tour "normal" state of mind.

Snap out of it and step out of the time into the present and *"just be and enjoy being"*, as Eckhart recommends:

> *"You might say, 'What a dreadful day,' without realizing that the cold, the wind, and the rain or whatever condition you react to are not dreadful. They 'are as they are'.*
>
> *What is dreadful is only your reaction and inner resistance to it, and the emotion created by this resistance."*

INNER TRANSFORMATION

Inner transformation can only take place here and now. You cannot postpone it without losing it. Regarding this transformation, the Indian philosopher and spiritual teacher Jiddu Krishnamurti (1895-1986) sustained in his celebrated book *"The First and Last Freedom"*:

> *"Transformation is in the future, can never be in the future. It can only be now, from moment to moment... When you see that something is false, that false thing drops away... As we are surrounded by so much that is false, perceiving the falseness from moment to moment is transformation.*

EXERCISE 6: SURRENDERING TO THE NOW

"Let me summarize the process. Focus your attention on the feeling inside you... Don't think about it - don't let the feeling turn into thinking. Don't judge or analyze... Be aware not only of the emotional pain but also of 'the one who observes,' the silent watcher. This is the power of the Now, the power of your own conscious presence. Then see what happens."

Eckhart Tolle

ACCORDING TO ECKHART TOLLE, surrendering to the Now means consciously accepting the present moment *"as it is"*. But not by passive resignation! It means ceasing to base your happiness on a *"cherished future"* or a *"cherished past"* and ending all resistance to the Now, as he briefly indicates:

> **"The basis for effective action is to come into an inner alignment with the 'is-ness' of this moment: This is how it is."**

This inner alignment has been known for centuries and received many names.

Jesus called it surrendering our will to God by accepting that *"Thy will be done on earth as it is on heaven."*

Meister Eckhart defined it as *"letting go of one self"* through the cessation of **self**-will and the gradual acquirement of what he called an *"empty spirit"*.

Carl Jung called it *"the art of letting things happen"* and highlighted its importance for the healthy mind:

> **"The art of letting things happen, action through nonaction, letting go of oneself, as taught by Meister Eckhart, became for me the key opening the door to the way.**

> **"We must let things happen in our psyche. For us, it is actually an art of which scarce persons know anything. Consciousness is incessantly interfering."**

Last but not least *A Course in Miracles,* which Eckhart practiced back in London during his beginning days as spiritual teacher and still recommends to those in need of higher understanding, calls this *"placing the future in the Hands of God"* (your inner Divinity or Ultimate Reality) and bases this transcendental experience on following these three steps:

FIRST:

Recognize that God holds your future as He holds your past and present:

> *"They are one to Him, and so they should be one to you. Yet in this world, the temporal progression still seem as real. And therefore you are not asked to understand the lack of sequence really found in time."*

SECOND:

Instead of trying to control your life leave everything in God´s Hands:

> *"You are only asked to let the future go and place it in God's Hands. And you'll see by experience that you have laid the past and present in His Hands as well, for the past will punish you no more, and future dread will now be meaningless.*
>
> *"Release the future, for the past is gone. And what is present, freed from its bequest of grief and misery, of pain and loss, becomes the instant in which time escapes the bondage of illusions,*

where it runs its pitiless, inevitable course... Place, then, your future in the Hands of God...."

THIRD:

Repeat to yourself several times a day or as often as you can the following statement, especially each time you catch your *"voice in the head"* repeating a negative and undesired thought or if you find yourself irremediably lost in a continuous and pessimistic mental conversation or chatter:

"I place the future in the Hands of God"

TO EACH DAY ITS OWN TROUBLES

According to his celebrated *Sermon of the Mount,* Jesus metaphorically stressed the importance of freeing ourselves from the trap of time and ceasing to worry about the future by surrendering to *"what is"*:

"So this I say to you, do not worry about your life, what you will eat or what you will drink; nor about your body or what you will wear. Is not your life worth more than your food and your body more than your clothes?

"Watch the birds of the skies, for they neither plant nor obtain nor gather in barns. And yet your heavenly Father feeds them. Are you not worth more than they? Which of you can add a single cubit to his height? So why do you worry about clothing?

"Contemplate the lilies of the field and how they grow: they neither work nor weave; and yet I say to you that even Solomon in all his glory never did dressed like one of these!"

"Now if God so dresses the meadow of the field, which today grows and tomorrow burns in the furnace, will He not dress you better, O men of poor faith?

"Therefore stop worrying and saying: 'What will we eat?' or 'What will we drink?' or 'What will we wear?' Gentiles seek these things. But your heavenly Father knows what you need. So first seek the kingdom of God and His righteousness, and all these things will be added to you.

"So cease to worry about tomorrow, for tomorrow will worry about its own things. Enough for the day is its own trouble!"

VII: EXPERIENCING THE JOY OF LIVING

"As soon as you honor the present moment, all unhappiness and struggle dissolve, and life begins to flow with joy and ease."

Eckhart Tolle

THE SEVENTH STEP OF STOPPING NEGATIVE THINKING consists in learning to experience the Joy of Living.

As the XIV Dalai Lama admits, the biggest difference between common westerners and Tibetan lamas as well as the biggest difference is that we constantly experience what the lamas call *"ceaseless streams of thoughts"*, just like they do, only that they *"choose not to listen"*:

> *"Even the high Lamas of Tibet experience the ceaseless stream of thoughts running through our minds. The only difference is, we don't listen."*

Similarly, an ancient Chinese proverb has anonymously claimed for thousands of years:

> *"You cannot prevent the birds of sorrow from flying over your head, but you can prevent them from building nests in your hair."*

This ancestral metaphor symbolizes that we cannot avoid having negative thoughts every now and then. However, we can learn to ignore them as soon as they appear in our minds by consciously avoiding in these cases to engage yourself in useless "inner chat" with the voice in your head - thus stopping the *"birds of sorrow"* from *"building nests in your hair"*.

THE CREATIVE USE OF MIND

Now that you have learned how to slow down your flow of thoughts and avoid the traps of repetitive negative thinking, you are free to use your mind creatively in your daily life, when solving problems, making a decision or overcoming obstacles, as Eckhart explains:

> *"If you need to use your mind for a specific purpose, use it in conjunction with your inner body. Only if you are able to be conscious without thought can you use your mind creatively, and the easiest way to enter that state is through your body.*

> *"Whenever an answer, a solution, or a creative idea is needed, stop thinking for a moment by focusing attention on your inner energy field. Become aware of the stillness.*

"When you resume thinking, it will be fresh and creative. In any thought activity, make it a habit to go back and forth every few minutes or so between thinking and an inner kind of listening, an inner stillness.

"Don't just think with your head, think with your whole body."

THE SECRET OF HAPPINESS

The problem with most people is that they believe themselves to be dependent on what happens for their own happiness.

On the contrary, as announced around half a century ago by the Indian enlightened spiritual teacher Jiddu Krishnamurti, you can experience happiness here and now as long as you avoid caring about what happens and simply accept the present moment *"as it is"*.

This is one way of saying that above all we need to turn the Now into our dear friend instead of our dark enemy, in alignment with *"what is"*, as Eckhart details:

"When we befriend the present moment with acceptance and non-resistance, we will feel more peaceful and be less torn by what we like and don't like. To be happier, make friends with what is...

"Accept the present moment and find the perfection that is deeper than any form and untouched by time...

"The joy of Being, which is the only true happiness, cannot come to you through any form, possession, achievement, person, or event—through anything that happens.

"That joy cannot come to you—ever. It emanates from the formless dimension within you, from consciousness itself and thus is One With Who You Are."

EXERCISE 7: BEATING NEGATIVE THINKING

"For some, the awakening happens as they suddenly become aware of the kinds of thoughts they habitually think, especially persistent negative thoughts that they may have been identified with all of their lives. Suddenly there is an awareness that is aware of thought but is not part of it."

Eckhart Tolle

THE FOLLOWING STEPS condense the basic teachings presented in this book, designed to help you beat pessimism and adequately face negative obstacles and casualties with the *Power of Now*:

FIRST:

The next time you find yourself facing times of trouble and adversity, do not despair! Begin by avoiding all impulsive reactions and take a deep breath instead.

Become the Watcher of your thoughts as you breathe and avoid blindly following the negative impulses that may arise, which are always pre-determined by what Eckhart Tolle calls *"unconscious mental-emotional reactive patterns."*

A single deep breath will help you increase your alertness and interrupt your *"inner chat"*, as Eckhart advices:

"This can start with a very simple thing, such as taking one conscious breath... so that there is no mental commentary running at the same time..."

SECOND:

Remember that *"you are what you think"* and that instead of perceiving *"reality as it is"* your thinking mind always interprets everything in terms of *"what you think it is"*. Avoid reacting based on the *"illusory sense of how you should react"* and instead of blindly repeating your usual negative patterns, concentrate on following your breaths.

THIRD:

Keep breathing consciously and closely observing your *"voice in the head"*. No matter what it says or how it reacts, avoid getting hooked on mental dialogues and watch out for any *"repetitive thinking patterns"*, which Eckhart describes as *"those old audiotapes that have been playing in your head perhaps for many years."*

FOURTH:

As you continue breathing consciously, accept your present situation without getting stuck in it and realize that it is completely natural for things not to always necessarily turn out as expected. So stop reacting immaturely and do your best to see the glass half-full instead of half-empty, as Eckhart suggests:

> *"It is true that my present life situation is the result of things that happened in the past, but it is still my present situation, and being stuck in it is what makes me unhappy."*

FIFTH:

Avoid thinking about a better future or past and their countless *"what ifs"* by concentrating in the Now. Do not compare your present situation with an imagined reality, no matter what, for this always postpones your own happiness instead of allowing you to experience the joy of Being right here and now.

SIXTH:

Turn to the inner energy gently vibrating within your hand and sink in the Now without resistance, accepting that this always leads to a *"higher understanding of things"* compatible with taking action, solving problems and accomplishing immediate goals.

SEVENTH:

Finally, feel your inner feeling of aliveness growing within you and filling your whole body with a *"subtle emanation of joy arising from deep within"*, as Eckhart notes:

> **"When these gaps occur, you feel a certain stillness and peace inside you. This is the beginning of your natural state of felt oneness with Being, which is usually obscured by the mind.**
>
> **"With practice, the sense of stillness and peace will deepen. In fact, there is no end to its depth. You will also feel a subtle emanation of joy arising from deep within: the joy of Being."**

Your inner aliveness is the gateway to the joy of Living. Feel it silently vibrating within you. Do you sense its aliveness? Can you feel the subtle joy?

Yes, it is time to give yourself permission to be happy here and now! You deserve it! It is your right!

Remain in the gap and focus on experiencing the joy of Being vibrating within you and flowing from your heart!

There is no longer need to keep waiting to experience happiness. So forget your self-imposed barriers and excuses! Start being happy here and now!

It is time to awaken!

Open your eyes and realize that, no matter what, everything is perfect! Better impossible, for nothing exists other than the Now!

Remain in the gap as long as you can and repeat this each day as many times as you decide and begin to experience your inner transformation with the Power of Now!

ABOUT THE AUTHOR

IN MY OWN WORDS

A. J. PARR is a journalist, Comparative Religion researcher and indie author with a lifelong interest and experience in meditation techniques:

I RECEIVED MY FIRST HINDU INITIATION when I was 17 years old (I am now 58), in the *Mission of the Divine Light,* founded back in the 70s by Guru Maharaj Ji (presently known as *Prem Rawat*). His basic teachings included four different meditation techniques to stop the mind and free us from Illusion.

I was almost 30 when I received my second Hindu initiation and meditation technique, this time from a disciple of Maharishi

Mahesh Yogi (1918-2008), creator of Transcendental Meditation or TM. It must be said that Maharishi´s *"mantra meditation"* technique was practiced, among others, by the Beatles, Mia Farrow, Shirley MacLaine, Donovan, and also Deepak Chopra, who worked side by side with Maharishi before starting his own career a spiritual guide. That year I also joined the Freemasonry and continued in its files until obtaining, several years later, the Sublime Degree of Master Mason

At the age of 37, I received my third Eastern initiation and meditation technique, this time from the Sant Mat tradition, also known as *"The Path of Saints"*, derived from Hinduism and Sikhism.

Finally, during the last decade, I have studied *"A Course in Miracles"* together with the teachings of Eckhart Tolle, Deepak Chopra, Dalai Lama, Ramana Maharshi and Krishnamurti, among others, experiencing the inner transformation and understanding that finally gave birth to *"The Secret of Now Series"*. **Contact the author at:** edicionesdelaparra@gmail.com

THANKS IN ADVANCE!

Let us rejoice and contemplate eternity! Namaste!

A. J.   P A R R

PUBLISHED BY:

GRAPEVINE BOOKS
EDICIONES DE LA PARRA

Made in the USA
Lexington, KY
29 May 2017